T0057059

Allegretto (𝅗𝅥 = 𝅗𝅥.)
fp
p
p
p

VIOLIN

FANTASIA ON
GREENSLEEVES

Arranged for Violin and Pianoforte by
MICHAEL MULLINAR

R. VAUGHAN WILLIAMS

VIOLIN

Copyright in U.S.A. and all countries, 1944 Oxford University Press
Printed in Great Britain
OXFORD UNIVERSITY PRESS, MUSIC DEPARTMENT, GREAT CLARENDON STREET, OXFORD OX2 6DP
Photocopying this copyright material is ILLEGAL.

f
p
cresc.
cresc.
rall.
f
p
rall.

Lento
p
p
Lento moderato
p
p
pp

p cantabile
pp
ppp
Ped.

OXFORD
UNIVERSITY PRESS

ISBN 978-0-19-359307-7